UNDERSTANDING
WORLD RELIGIONS

Understanding Christianity

Don Nardo

ReferencePoint
Press®

San Diego, CA

© 2019 ReferencePoint Press, Inc.
Printed in the United States

For more information, contact:
ReferencePoint Press, Inc.
PO Box 27779
San Diego, CA 92198
www.ReferencePointPress.com

LIBRARY OF CONGRESS CATALOGING-IN-PUBLICATION DATA

Name: Nardo, Don, 1947– author.
Title: Understanding Christianity/by Don Nardo.
Description: San Diego: ReferencePoint Press, 2018. | Series: Understanding World Religions | Includes bibliographical references and index.
Identifiers: LCCN 2017057451 (print) | LCCN 2017059473 (ebook) | ISBN 9781682824627 (eBook) | ISBN 9781682824610 (hardback)
Subjects: LCSH: Christianity.
Classification: LCC BR121.3 (ebook) | LCC BR121.3 .N36 2018 (print) | DDC 230—dc23
LC record available at https://lccn.loc.gov/2017057451

CONTENTS

World Religions: By the Numbers

According to a 2017 Pew Research Center demographic analysis, Christians were the largest religious group in the world in 2015. However, that may be changing. The same analysis projects Muslims to be the world's fastest-growing major religious group over the next four decades.

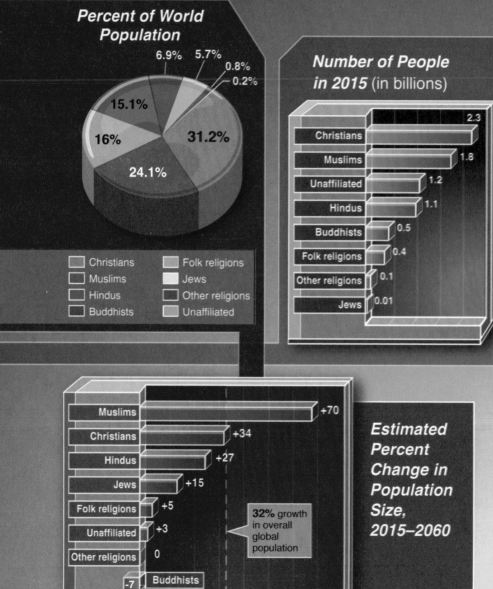

Percent of World Population

- 6.9%
- 5.7%
- 0.8%
- 0.2%
- 15.1%
- 16%
- 31.2%
- 24.1%

Legend:
- Christians
- Muslims
- Hindus
- Buddhists
- Folk religions
- Jews
- Other religions
- Unaffiliated

Number of People in 2015 (in billions)

Religion	Number
Christians	2.3
Muslims	1.8
Unaffiliated	1.2
Hindus	1.1
Buddhists	0.5
Folk religions	0.4
Other religions	0.1
Jews	0.01

Estimated Percent Change in Population Size, 2015–2060

Muslims	+70
Christians	+34
Hindus	+27
Jews	+15
Folk religions	+5
Unaffiliated	+3
Other religions	0
Buddhists	-7

32% growth in overall global population

Source: Conrad Hackett and David McClendon, "Christians Remain World's Largest Religious Group, but They Are Declining in Europe," Pew Research Center: The Changing Global Religious Landscape, April 5, 2017. www.pewresearch.org.

INTRODUCTION

Christianity's Eternal Mission

Shortly after assuming the position of leader of the Roman Catholic Church in March 2013, Pope Francis delivered his first address. Francis sincerely thanked the cardinals, bishops, and many other Catholics for the good wishes they had extended to him after he was elected.

The new pope also devoted a fairly large portion of the speech to the theme of evangelism. Also known as missionary work, it consists of attempts by church representatives to convert non-Catholics to Catholicism. Francis spoke of

> announcing in a convincing way that Christ is the one savior of the whole of man and of all men. This announcement is as valid today as it was at the beginning of Christianity when the Church worked for the great missionary expansion of the gospel [account of Jesus's teachings]. All together, pastors and faithful, we will make an effort to respond faithfully to the eternal mission: to bring Jesus Christ to humanity, and to lead humanity to an encounter with Jesus Christ.[1]

In a separate speech given that same week, Francis emphasized the same theme. "Building the church" through missionary work, he said, must be a primary goal of Catholics. "We speak of stones," he continued. "Stones are solid. But living stones, stones anointed by the Holy Spirit. Building the Church, the Bride of Christ, on the cornerstone that is the Lord himself. This is another kind of movement in our lives: building."[2] To expand the church's influence and ministry, Francis stated, Catholic Christians must repeatedly profess, or tell about, Jesus and his teachings.

Billions of Believers

Catholics are not the only Christians who engage in missionary work in an effort to gain new converts to the teachings of Jesus. There are also Protestant evangelists, for instance. Together, Catholics, Protestants, and other groups who revere and worship Jesus Christ make up the enormous worldwide Christian religion. In fact, Christianity is at present the world's largest religion, with close to forty thousand separate Christian denominations (sometimes also known as sects or ministries). Experts on religion report that the total number of Christians now exceeds 2 billion people.

> *"Christ is the one savior of the whole of man and of all men."*[1]
> —Pope Francis

A brief look at the three biggest Christian groups partly reveals how the faith expanded and divided over the centuries. By far the oldest denomination, the Catholic Church, formally emerged during the fourth century CE. Also the biggest single Christian organization, it boasts roughly 1.2 billion members, or more than half of all Christians.

Despite its long-standing top ranking, Catholicism lost numerous adherents during the Protestant Reformation. Often dated from 1517 to the mid-1600s, the Reformation was a movement in which many European Catholics quit the church and founded their own ministries. (The term *Protestant* derives from the fact that they were protesting various aspects of Catholicism.) Modern Protestant groups number in the thousands and have more than 700 million followers.

The third-largest Christian organization today is closely related to Catholicism, which was western Rome's official faith when its empire collapsed during the late 400s CE. The realm's eastern sector, with its capital of Constantinople on the Black Sea's southern rim, survived and morphed into the Greek-speaking Byzantine Empire. The Byzantine, or Eastern Orthodox, version of Christianity shares many beliefs and customs with Catholicism. Eastern Orthodox Christians number around 260 million.

Spreading the Good News About Jesus

No matter which denomination they may belong to, all Christians agree on certain central, fundamental beliefs and practices. They

Pope Francis blesses pilgrims in St. Peter's Square in 2014. Francis has taken many opportunities to remind the faithful that the Catholic Church must continually expand its influence through missionary work and spreading the teachings of Jesus Christ.

all revere Jesus's ethical teachings, for example. As for practices, all Christians support evangelism in one form or another. They believe they can make the world a better place by converting others to Christianity. This missionary belief and practice is rooted in the New Testament portion of the Bible. Years after Jesus's passing, his famous follower Paul remarked, "The gospel is bearing fruit and growing throughout the whole world." He added, "Pray for us as well that God will open to us a door for the word, that we may declare the mystery of Christ [to all people], so that I may reveal it clearly, as I should."[3]

After Paul's time, as small Christian communities spread across the Roman Empire, Christian spokesmen arose who tried to explain and defend Christian beliefs and customs to non-Christians.

Steadily, their activities, which expanded knowledge of Christianity, evolved into a concerted effort.

Ever since the ancient era, therefore, Christian missionaries have followed the custom of going forth into the world. Their goal has been to spread what they call the good news about Jesus and his teachings. Evangelists employ a wide range of methods as part of this effort. The most basic one, which is still widely used, is to travel from town to town and go door to door. Some missionaries spread the word in large-scale rallies attended by tens of thousands of people. Also, in modern times missionary work is frequently accomplished through media and entertainment venues—which attract millions. Television ministries, including Catholic versions and many different Protestant versions, have been familiar fare since that electronic technology emerged during the late 1940s and early 1950s.

The Mission Continues

Using all of these various methods Christian missionaries have spread their faith to all corners of the globe. Millions of non-Christians were converted in Africa, Asia, and elsewhere. Still, more than three-quarters of the world's population of about 7.6 billion (in 2017) remains non-Christian, so the work of Christian missionaries continues.

> "We were created to use our lives as an instrument . . . to extend God's Kingdom."[4]
>
> —Protestant pastor Sunday Adelaja

This task, which has long been one of the faith's principal attributes, is regularly advocated by Christian leaders. From the head of the largest denomination, Pope Francis, to those in charge of the tiniest, least-known Christian groups, all of these individuals agree on both the spirit and implementation of evangelism. Sunday Adelaja, who leads one of the planet's smallest Christian ministries, the Ukraine-based Embassy of the Blessed Kingdom of God for All Nations, sums up the missionary spirit. "We were created to use our lives as an instrument and everything we have to extend God's Kingdom," he says. "Don't wait for people to locate *you*. Rather, reach out to people and help to bring *them* to Christ."[4]

CHAPTER ONE

The Origins of Christianity

Christianity's beginnings are sometimes erroneously said to date to the lifetime and teachings of the first-century CE Jewish preacher Jesus of Nazareth. His life and ideas are certainly central to the faith. The reality, however, is that the seeds for his ministry, and the later religion largely based on it, had already been planted by the time of his birth.

That now-famous birth took place in about 5 or 4 BCE in what later became the Roman province of Judea (in 6 CE), today occupied by the modern nation of Israel. Jesus's ideas and those of his followers were shaped partly by the local Jewish religious concepts and customs of that age. They were also influenced by Syrian, Greek, Roman, and other spiritual ideas then floating through the area of the Middle East bordering the Mediterranean Sea.

Jesus and the new faith his followers later established could not help but be influenced by that complex religious melting pot. As a result, much of what he preached during his lifetime was neither unique nor revolutionary. Many years after his death, however, Christianity did bring about a major revolution in religious thought and practice that affected the course of human civilization. The late noted historian Michael Grant aptly called it "one of the few revolutions in the world's history that has lasted."[5]

The Influences of the Mystery Cults

Among the elements of the eastern Mediterranean religious melting pot that came to shape Christianity were those of a number of so-called mystery cults. These religions filtered into the Greco-Roman sphere from the Middle East during the last two centuries

BCE. (The term *mystery* derived from those faiths' secret initiation ceremonies; typically the initiations of a given mystery cult were witnessed strictly by members of that group.)

Among those eastern-born cults, the oldest and perhaps most popular was that of the nature goddess Cybele, known as "the Great Mother," from Anatolia (now Turkey). It was eventually revealed that her initiation ceremony involved the ritual slaughter and sacrifice (offering to the goddess) of a bull. Splashing that sacred animal's blood on an initiate was thought to cause him or her to be reborn as an accepted member of the faith.

Other prominent mystery cults were those of Mithras, from Persia (now Iran), and the Egyptian goddess Isis. In his novel *The Golden Ass*, the second-century CE Roman writer Apuleius describes a sacred gathering of Isis's followers during one of the cult's annual festivals. Swarms of those followers, he writes,

> came surging along, men and women of every rank and age, gleaming with linen garments spotlessly white. The women had sprayed their hair with perfume, and [the] men had shaved their heads completely, so that their bald pates shone. With their rattles of bronze, silver, and even gold, they made a shrill, tinkling sound. Accompanying them were [the] priests of the cult, who were drawn from the ranks of famed nobility. They wore white linen garments. [Behind them came] a cow rearing upright, the fertile representation of the goddess who is mother of all.[6]

Early Christianity had several customs similar to those of these mystery religions. Like Mithras's followers, for instance, the Christians held dear a child's miraculous birth, practiced baptism, and believed that people's souls would survive death. "The promise of an afterlife for the initiated would have been commonplace to anyone who had contact with mystery religions," scholar Charles Freeman points out. In fact, a fair amount of the religious imagery in the Christian New Testament reflects that of the mystery cults. Freeman cites the example of Christian reverence for Mary, the mother of Jesus. That reverence "acquires a new richness when placed in parallel with the worship of other mother figures in these [mystery] religions."[7]

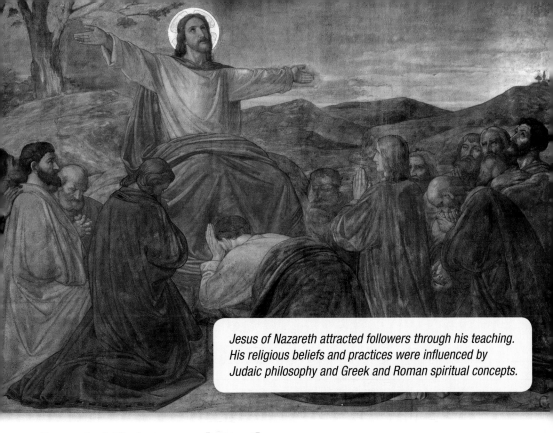

Jesus of Nazareth attracted followers through his teaching. His religious beliefs and practices were influenced by Judaic philosophy and Greek and Roman spiritual concepts.

Jesus's Ministry and Death

Even more influential on early Christianity was the religion from which it sprang—Judaism, the faith of the Jews. So-called Judeo-Christian religious culture was, and still is, built upon the concept that the Christian god and the Hebrew god of the Old Testament are one and the same deity. Also, the two faiths shared the same ethical tradition. That tradition stresses showing respect for parents and other elders; having sexual relations only when married; and providing compassion and charity to the poor and sick.

In addition, the early Christians preserved numerous Jewish customs, including assigning the faith's leadership to a group of male elders. Particularly important among Christian borrowings from Judaism was the Old Testament, which became the first section of the Christian Bible. It recounts many moving tales of the adventures of prophets like Moses and the subsequent establishment of the ancient Hebrew kingdom of Israel and Palestine.

A rich Jewish cultural and religious tradition therefore predated and provided a basis for Jesus Christ, his teachings, and the later development of the Christian faith. (His given name was Jesus; the name *Christ* came from the Greek word *Christos*, meaning

The prophet Moses received the Ten Commandments from God to instruct others on key religious laws. Moses's Story is part of the Old Testament, a series of books that early Christians borrowed from the Hebrew Bible.

"messiah" or "anointed one," and was used by his followers only after his death.) Most people are familiar with the story that Jesus was a Jewish carpenter's son who, in his youth, began preaching among fellow Jewish residents of Judea.

Among Jesus's primary messages was an emphasis on the ancient Jewish tradition of love and of charity for society's poor and downtrodden. "Blessed are the meek," he said, "for they shall inherit the earth." Moreover, "blessed are they who hunger and thirst for righteousness, for they will be satisfied."[8] Another of Jesus's main messages had long been promoted by other Jewish preachers, including John the Baptist, the wandering holy man who had baptized Jesus in the Jordan River. That message prophesied that the kingdom of God was so imminent that it might arrive at any moment. The preachers described this so-called kingdom as a utopian age in which God would vanquish the enemies of the Jews, who would thereafter enjoy eternal salvation in a world swept clean of evil.

In and of themselves, such ideas were not unusual. Jesus, however, got into trouble with the local Jewish and Roman authorities partly because he had gained an increasingly large following of people of all walks of life. Also, some of his followers started suggesting that he might be the Messiah. Jewish tradition had long predicted that this superior being, sent by God, would materialize and rescue the Jews from the oppression they had suffered at the hands of many other peoples over prior centuries. In addition, a few of Jesus's followers went so far as to suggest he might be God's son.

> *"Blessed are the meek, for they shall inherit the earth."[8]*
>
> —Jesus

These events and ideas did not sit well with the Judean authorities, who came to see Jesus and his core followers—the disciples (or apostles)—as a possible threat to the established order. As a result, Jesus was arrested sometime between 30 and 33 CE. Within a few weeks at most, the Roman official in charge of Judea sentenced the prisoner to be executed via crucifixion, then a common form of capital punishment.

The People of the Way

Certain key events that occurred after Jesus's execution turned out to be the principal pillars atop which the Christian faith was erected. First, soon after his body was interred in a rock-lined tomb outside Jerusalem, some of his followers claimed he had risen from the dead. For at least some people, this seemed to confirm that he was indeed the Messiah and son of God.

Based largely on this claim of Jesus's resurrection, his small but loyal core following remained intact. The disciples and some other adherents began preaching that Jesus would soon return to usher in God's kingdom and thereby liberate the Jews from Rome. Not surprisingly, this message was initially aimed solely at Jews. After all, Jesus's followers still considered themselves to be Jews and practiced the usual Jewish rituals, including observing certain dietary laws and circumcising young males. At first numbering no more than a couple hundred members, they called themselves the people of "the Way." Most other Jews

Although a number of gentiles joined the Christian community during the 50s and early 60s CE, Jewish Christians still retained a major voice. That changed fairly quickly after the Jews in Judea rebelled against Rome during the late 60s. The revolt culminated in the Roman sack of Jerusalem in 70. Most of the Jewish Christians died in the bloody turmoil. The survivors fled, and evidence suggests that a few of them took refuge in the deserts east of Judea, and elsewhere. A few small pockets of Jewish Christians remained intact in what is today Jordan and Syria until at least 300 CE. Known as Ebionites, they developed a number of distinct beliefs different from those of what would become mainstream Christianity. For instance, they held that Jesus became God's son only when he was baptized in the Jordan River by John. When Jesus "came up from the water," a surviving Ebionite writing states, "the heavens were opened, and he saw [God] in the likeness of a dove that descended and entered into him. And a voice from heaven said 'You are my beloved son, [and] in you I am well pleased.'" The Ebionites and other surviving Jewish Christians became increasingly fragmented and over time died out.

Early Christian Writings, "Gospel of the Ebionites." www.earlychristianwritings.com.

distrusted them. A few even persecuted them, insisting that those who claimed that their dead leader was divine were uttering falsehoods and dishonoring God.

The next key event in Christianity's formation occurred in 36 CE. It consisted of the conversion of Saul of Tarsus, later called Paul, to the Way. A Jew who at first persecuted Jesus's followers, Paul suddenly changed his mind. In an account that later became part of the New Testament, he claimed that one day he was in the midst of a trip to Syria when suddenly "a light from heaven flashed about him. And he fell to the ground and heard a voice saying to him, 'Saul, Saul, why do you persecute me?' And he said, 'Who are you, Lord?' And he said, 'I am Jesus, whom you are persecuting; but rise and enter the city, and you will be told what to do."[9]

Paul soon dedicated himself to a new and unusual project. It involved bringing the good news of Jesus's offer of salvation to the gentiles, or non-Jews, a move he reasoned would significantly increase the chances of gaining new converts. He realized that most gentiles would be reluctant to join a Jewish religious sect and follow Jewish rituals and customs. Few, if any, non-Jews were willing to circumcise themselves, for example. So Paul wisely eliminated these requirements for gentiles. The group's other elders agreed to those terms around the year 49.

By that time they called themselves Christians, after the name *Christ*. According to the New Testament's book of Acts, Jewish members of the group who dwelled in the Syrian city of Antioch first coined the term. For several more years Jewish Christians continued to prosper beside their gentile brethren. That changed drastically, however, when most Jewish Christians were killed during the Roman capture and sack of Jerusalem in 70.

New Generations of Leaders

By about 100 CE the Christians had largely separated from Judaism, although the new faith did retain many Jewish beliefs, practices, and sacred writings. The Christians also started moving outward from the eastern Mediterranean region. A little at a time they established new communities of the faithful in Greece, Italy, Spain, North Africa, and elsewhere.

After Paul and the last few original Christian leaders died, those who succeeded them stressed missionary work as a way of gaining as many new members as possible. Among these church elders was Ignatius of Antioch. He penned letters to all the Christian communities, stressing unity. Ignatius also coined the term *Catholic* (from a word meaning "wide-ranging" or "all-embracing") and suggested that each community should be headed by a leader called a bishop

> *"Let no man do anything connected with the Church without the bishop."*[10]
>
> —Ignatius of Antioch

(from the Greek word *episkopos*, meaning "overseer"). "See that you all follow the bishop, even as Jesus Christ does the Father," he said. "Let no man do anything connected with the Church without the bishop." Furthermore, "it is not lawful without the bishop either to baptize or to celebrate a love-feast; but whatsoever he shall approve of, that is also pleasing to God, so that everything that is done may be secure and valid."[10]

In the three generations that followed Ignatius, the bishops were often aided by prominent Christian spokesmen who explained their faith to non-Christians. Some of the better known of their number included Tertullian, Justin, and Origen. Well educated and well spoken, they made it their mission not only to explain Christian beliefs, but also to call for treating Christians tolerantly.

The Persecutions

These efforts were badly needed because many Romans, including most Roman leaders, viewed Christians as either antisocial troublemakers or criminals, or both. Indeed, the Christian community came to bear the awful dishonor of being seen as having *odium generis humani*, Latin for "hatred for the human race."[11] The late classical scholar Harold Mattingly pointed out some of the reasons for this terrible reputation. The Christians, he wrote, refused to worship the multiple gods that most Romans embraced, instead "insisting on the supremacy of one god of their own." Moreover, the Christians "were inclined to abstain from the good things of life—from theaters, banquets, shows of amphitheater and circus. More than this, they were suspected of horrible crimes, [among them] child murder."[12] The latter charge was based on false rumors that Christian rituals, usually held in secret, included sacrificing and eating babies.

> *"[Christians] were inclined to abstain from the good things of life."*[12]
>
> —Historian Harold Mattingly

Another black mark against the Christians was that they refused to take part in emperor worship. Although few Romans actually believed their emperors were divine, both custom and law allowed those leaders to claim such special status. Hence, nearly all Romans occasionally, if sometimes reluctantly, took part in that custom. The followers of Jesus were the exception, and the Roman government viewed their refusal as a potential threat to public order.

These and other charges leveled against the Christians made it easier for Roman authorities to carry out anti-Christian persecutions during the first three centuries CE. Members of the faith variously suffered beatings; arrest and temporary imprisonment; sentences of execution, often in public arenas; and the burning of their meeting places and sacred writings. The largest persecution took place in 303 at the instigation of the emperor Galerius. All across the eastern half of the Roman Empire, where Galerius held sway, the government closed down Christian churches, forbade Christians to meet for worship, and burned their religious writings.

Protection, Legitimacy, and Triumph

This assault on the Christians turned out to be the last of the persecutions. Very soon after enduring widespread outrages, they suddenly came under the protection of a new, more humane emperor—Constantine I. He and his father, Constantius, coruled the empire's western sector while Galerius ruled the eastern. The father and son had both refused to take part in the persecution, seeing it as unfair and mean-spirited. Constantine proceeded to befriend a number of prominent Christians. He also came to see

In the first two centuries CE, Roman emperors routinely persecuted Christians for their refusal to worship Roman gods. In 313 CE, Constantine I (left) became the first emperor to protect Christians and sanction their beliefs.

One of the sweeping changes brought about by the Christians' rapid rise to power during the fourth-century Roman world was the erection of numerous churches. According to classical scholar Charles Freeman,

> All over the Empire new churches appeared, resplendent with their fine decoration. Many were built over the shrines of martyrs, places which had been venerated since the early days of the [Christian faith]. Others took over prime sites within the major cities—even the sites of earlier imperial palaces. [Churches] now became magnificent treasure houses, objects of awe and inspiration of worship. [For their design] there was a pagan model to copy: the basilica, typically a long hall with a flat timber roof and aisles running along its length. For centuries the basilicas had been used as law courts, with [public officials] enthroned at one end, [and] as markets. [Now] they were to receive a new function. For the church, the basilica model was ideal. The clergy or bishop could be installed at one end, as the [Roman official] had been, and large numbers of worshipers could fit inside. The greatest of the basilicas was St. Peter's in Rome, constructed over the shrine [thought] to be the resting place of St. Peter's body.

Charles Freeman, *The World of the Romans.* New York: Oxford University Press, 1993, p. 162.

the Christian god as either an ally of or one and the same as his own favorite god, the Unconquered Sun. (Worship of that deity was another of the several eastern mystery cults that had long been popular in the Roman world.)

For these and other reasons, Constantine decided to legitimize the Christians and their faith by granting them legal protection. It took the form of a decree of toleration, forged in 313 by himself and Licinius, who had succeeded Galerius as the eastern emperor. The so-called Edict of Milan said in part that the government now gave "all Christians freedom of choice to follow the ritual which they wish."[13]

Constantine's support for the Christians never waned. In the years that followed, he frequently mediated disputes that arose among the bishops. Also, in 330 he established a new city that he dedicated specifically to the Christian god and Jesus's mother, Mary—Constantinople, "the city of Constantine," located on the Bosphorus Strait just south of the Black Sea. In addition, Constantine sponsored the building of numerous Christian churches. As a final gesture of support for the Christians, he formally converted to the faith on his deathbed in 337.

Thereafter, Christianity underwent rapid and spectacular growth. Constantine's three sons were all devout Christians, as were all the Roman emperors who followed, save one (Julian, who reigned from 361 to 363). In the onrushing Christian tide, pagans (non-Christians) came increasingly under attack by zealous Christian bishops. The latter argued that God had purposely designed the Roman Empire as a place in which Christianity could grow. One by one, Christian emperors accepted such ideas, and by the 390s they had banned pagan sacrifices and closed all pagan temples.

"All Christians [now have] freedom of choice to follow the ritual which they wish."[13]

—The Edict of Milan

In less than a century Christianity had been transformed from a small, hated religious group on society's fringes to Rome's official religion. A triumph of staggering proportions, this turn of events gave Christian leaders tremendous power over the everyday lives and personal beliefs of tens of millions of people, including the emperors and other Roman officials. In fact, in many ways the government came to serve the church instead of the other way around.

Thus, when the western Roman government collapsed under the weight of massive invasions of European tribal peoples during the late 400s, the Christian church survived. Its missionaries soon brought the rest of Europe into the Christian fold. The faith initiated by Paul and a few other early devotees of Jesus, a group long reviled and persecuted, had become the spiritual guide for medieval and later modern Europe. The Christian revolution—unarguably one of history's most influential movements—was complete.

CHAPTER TWO

What Do Christians Believe?

A listing and basic explanation of all existing Christian beliefs would fill many volumes. In large part this is because so many different Christian denominations exist, and large numbers of them have certain beliefs peculiar to their own groups. For example, several of the beliefs of the Eastern Orthodox Church, centered in eastern Europe and Russia, are markedly different from those of Baptist congregations in the United States.

Still, the vast majority of Christians—in Russia, the United States, and around the globe—share a number of core beliefs. Moreover, most of those principles have remained largely unchanged since the faith's formative first four centuries. Some of these core beliefs, including the existence of a single, all-powerful god, derived from Judaism. Others were established in the writings of early Christian leaders or the texts making up the Old and New Testaments.

The Apostles' Creed and the Holy Trinity

An early important statement of some of Christianity's core beliefs, a list that emerged in Rome in around 150 CE, was at first labeled the Symbol of the Faith. No one knows exactly who penned it. But it seems to be a collection of ideas set down by a number of leading Christians during the two generations following St. Paul's death in about 67 CE. These early Christian writers are most often called the Apostolic Fathers. Thus, the list later came to be known as the Apostles' Creed.

That creed, or statement of belief, was intended to educate Christians in various parts of the Roman Empire. The goal was to inform the faithful of the beliefs a true Christian should hold and defend. To ensure that the message reached everyone, church fathers made the creed's three primary beliefs part of the baptism ceremony. Thereafter, every new member had to answer the following three questions:

Do you believe in God, the Father almighty? Do you believe in Christ Jesus, the Son of God, our Lord, who was born of the Holy Ghost [Spirit], who was crucified under Pontius Pilate, and died, and rose again at the third day, living from among the dead, and ascended into heaven and sat on the right of the Father and will come to judge the quick [the living] and the dead? Do you believe in the Holy Ghost, the holy church, and the resurrection of the flesh?[14]

Three different divine names are mentioned in the creed—Jesus, God, and the Holy Ghost. Together, almost all Christians believe, they make up the Holy Trinity. (Jehovah's Witnesses and

Pictured is a painting of the Holy Trinity from the Church of the Holy Sepulchre in Jerusalem. Some Christians accept that a single being can be composed of God, Jesus, and the Holy Ghost. Others believe that each of the three separate figures is a manifestation of the divinity of God.

Mormons are among the very few followers of Jesus who do not accept the trinity concept.) Many people, including large numbers of Christians, find the concept of the Trinity—three seemingly separate divine beings who are actually part of the same being—difficult to visualize or grasp. For this reason, the Trinity has long been referred to as one of the mysteries of the faith.

Regarding this truly mystifying concept, the early Christian writer Tertullian tried to explain it. God, he said, is "of one substance and of one condition, and of one power, inasmuch as He is one God, from whom these degrees and forms and aspects are reckoned, under the name of the Father, and of the Son, and of the Holy Ghost."[15] Two modern Christian writers go a bit further, saying that Christians do "not believe in three gods, but in one god in three persons." Furthermore,

> the divine persons are really distinct from one another. Father, Son, and Holy Spirit are not simply names for different aspects of God. Rather, they are distinct persons with distinct origins and special roles. God the Father is Creator or Source [of all things]; God the Son is Redeemer [saver of souls]; God the Holy Spirit is Advocate and Teacher.[16]

What God Initially Did

Of these three manifestations of God, Christians believe that God the Father fashioned the universe and everything in it, including humanity. Some Christians accept that he first created two people—Adam and Eve—who gave rise to all later humans. Other Christians think he more likely crafted various natural processes, including evolution, knowing they would produce humans over time.

In whatever manner God created people, Christians believe he did so out of a sense of divine love, and he wanted the people he made to multiply and prosper within the striking settings of the

Jesus's appearance to some of his followers after his death, as recorded in the New Testament, was not the only version of his direct postresurrection contacts with people. At least this is the belief of the Mormons, an offshoot of Christianity based in Utah. (Some mainstream Christians accept Mormons as fellow Christians, but others do not.) According to the Mormon scripture, the Book of Mormon, after his resurrection Jesus appeared to the Nephites in North America. (The Mormons claim the Nephites were descendants of a group of Jews who crossed the Atlantic and settled in America during the early 500s BCE.) The Book of Mormon says that Jesus interacted with and performed miracles for about twenty-five hundred Nephites:

> He said unto them: Blessed are ye because of your faith. And now behold, my joy is full. And when he had said these words, he wept, [and] he took their little children, one by one, and blessed them, and prayed unto the Father for them. [And] they cast their eyes towards heaven, and they saw the heavens open, and they saw angels descending out of heaven as it were in the midst of fire; and they came down and encircled those little ones about, [and] the angels did minister unto them.

3 Nephi 17:20–24, Book of Mormon.

natural world. What is more, God revealed his plans and hopes for humanity in the Hebrew scriptures and elsewhere. God further bestowed free will on people and expected them to use that gift prudently by making moral choices in their lives.

Christians also believe that, being all knowing, God was aware that at least some humans would *not* always make good choices. Some would likely commit sins of various kinds. The story of Adam and Eve's transgression (disobeying God when he forbade them to eat fruit from a specific tree) is widely thought by Christians to be the precedent, or model, of all the human sins that followed. Hence, it is frequently called the original sin. The fifth-century CE Christian writer Augustine held that all the people that followed those first two were tainted by that original sin; they must therefore perform certain rituals—particularly baptism—to rid themselves of it.

Also crucial in washing away human sins was Jesus's mission to the world. The aspect of the Trinity known as the Son took human form on Earth as Jesus, an occurrence that Christians call the Incarnation. Through his suffering, death, and resurrection, Christians believe Jesus made it possible for human sins to be forgiven. According to University of Oxford scholar Maurice Wiles,

> The story of [Jesus and his death on] the cross tells of his acceptance of the evil and the pain inflicted on him by human sinfulness even to the point of death. The story of the resurrection tells of the triumph over those forces of evil and over death. It is the power of that story, understood as something that God has done for humankind and for each individual within it, that has been the effective heart of the Christian message and of Christian belief. . . . [Jesus's] death was a sacrifice to do away with sin.[17]

Achieving Salvation

In the opinion of nearly all Christians, Jesus's resurrection also provided humans with a potential path to salvation. That is, thanks to his great sacrifice, they can survive the momentous watershed known as death and enjoy everlasting life in heaven. The resurrection is mentioned in various biblical passages. For instance, the Gospel of Mark says that three women—Mary Magdalene, Salome, and Mary, the mother of James— entered Jesus's tomb following his death. "They saw a young man sitting on the right side, dressed in a white robe, and they were amazed. 'Do not be amazed [he told them]. You seek Jesus of Nazareth, who was crucified. He has risen, he is not here. [Go] tell his disciples and Peter that he is going before you to Galilee. There you will see him.'"[18]

"*[Jesus's] death was a sacrifice to do away with sin.*"[17]

—University of Oxford scholar Maurice Wiles

Later, as the man in the tomb had foretold, Jesus appeared to the disciples at the Sea of Galilee, Christians believe. The Gospel

After his resurrection, Jesus appeared to Mary Magdalene in the garden outside his tomb. For many Christians, the revelation that Jesus was resurrected after death offers proof that death is not a finality.

of John states that Jesus said to them, "'Come and have breakfast.' Now none of the disciples dared to ask him, 'Who are you?' because they knew it was the Lord." In this way, "Jesus was revealed to the disciples after he was raised from the dead."[19]

These and other biblical passages recounting Jesus's appearances after his death are central to the faith because the resurrection is a major pillar of belief in virtually all Christian denominations. It is not simply the fact that Jesus himself conquered death that makes it so important. For Christians, this feat opened the door to

The exact manner in which believers will make it into heaven differs among Christians. Most mainstream Christians, including Catholics and most Protestants, assume that when the body dies the soul ascends into heaven in some manner. However, members of some conservative, fundamentalist Christian groups, including most Baptists and Congregationalists, believe in a major future event they call the "rapture."

They believe that not long before Jesus Christ's second coming (when he will judge humanity and usher in his long-predicted kingdom) God will take devout believers off the earth and meet them somewhere in the sky. This will supposedly happen in an instant, and those raptured in this manner will suddenly disappear, leaving their clothes behind in the spot in which they were sitting or standing. Those who advocate the rapture's reality claim it was predicted in this biblical passage: "[God] will come down from Heaven, with a loud command, with the voice of the archangel and with the trumpet call of God, and the dead in Christ will rise first. After that, we who are still alive and are left will be caught up together with them in the clouds to meet the Lord in the air."

First Thessalonians 4:16–17.

the possible resurrection of all members of the faith, as revealed in another key biblical passage. "If Christ is preached that he was raised from the dead," it states, "how can some of you say that there is no resurrection of the dead? But if there is no resurrection of the dead, then Christ has not been raised."[20] In other words, resurrection for all believers follows naturally from Jesus's own resurrection.

Salvation does not automatically occur. To achieve salvation a believer must be worthy of that privilege. Most Christian denominations hold that at the moment of death God judges each individual. After looking back at his or her life and deeds, he decides whether or not that person can enter heaven. Yet it is not merely doing good works that makes one worthy of salvation. One must also profess belief in only the Christian God.

In this regard, a majority of Christians around the world would almost certainly agree in principle with a statement of faith issued by the Presbyterian Church in September 2011. It says that "inherent goodness or admirable living" does not automatically qualify someone for entrance into heaven. Rather, it emphasizes that belief in Jesus and his message is paramount. Furthermore, one must not "assume that all people are saved regardless of faith."[21] In other words, the belief is that only through Christianity is salvation possible.

Heaven and Hell

Another cornerstone of Christian belief is that following death the human soul survives in some fashion. (Interestingly, although all Christian groups teach that an afterlife exists, not all of their followers accept that idea as fact. A 1999 study by the University of California, Los Angeles (UCLA), found that as many as 17 percent of self-described American Christians believe there is no afterlife.)

Nearly all Christian denominations hold that the afterlife can take several different forms, depending on the person. Those who are saved—that is, by God's grace achieve salvation—end up in heaven. As for what heaven is like, opinions vary widely among Christians. Some picture it as looking similar to Earth, with land, seas, mountains, and sky, except that it has no disease, crime, or worries. Other Christians view heaven in less specific terms. Although they accept its existence, they think it is too mysterious for humans to contemplate. Only when they arrive there will they appreciate what it is.

In whatever ways various Christians envision heaven's physical attributes, they all agree on one central point about that otherworldly place. Namely, God dwells there and upon arrival they will behold the Creator in all his glory. This gift—permission to see and know God—is called the beatific vision. According to Augustine (in his treatise *The City of God*), those who make it to heaven will "see and love, love and praise." After all, he goes on, "what other end do we propose to ourselves than to attain to the kingdom [of heaven] of which there is no end?"[22]

Another possible destination for souls after death, according to some Christian groups, including Catholicism, is purgatory. It is a kind of temporary stopping place, from which a person's soul may eventually go on to heaven. The most common view is that that person committed one or more minor sins in life; in purgatory, the person will do some kind of penance that will purify, or cleanse, him or her. At that point he or she can move on to heaven.

This fresco depicts the torment of sinners in Dante's version of hell. For some, hell is the destination of unrepentant sinners.

In contrast, the souls of people who committed more heinous sins in life, along with the spirits of unbelievers, end up in hell. Like heaven, hell has been envisioned in many different ways. Some Christians are convinced that in hell the souls of sinners suffer horrendous torments like those depicted by the fourteenth-century Italian writer Dante. In his famous *Divine Comedy*, he graphically describes those souls struggling in rivers of boiling blood, being perpetually eaten by hideous monsters, and their flesh seared in endlessly burning fires.

A majority of Christians, however, no longer view hell that way. Only 31 percent of American Christians said they did so in the 1999 UCLA study. A bigger proportion—37 percent—said they envisioned hell as simply the absence of God, which many Christians agree must be an awful fate for someone's soul. (The other 32 percent either suggested that hell consists of the soul's extinction, or nonexistence, or said they had no opinion on the matter.)

Beliefs Set Down in Writing

All of these fundamental and more or less universal Christian beliefs were based on and/or set down in the faith's key writings. Central to them is the Bible, the name of which comes from the Latin word *biblia*, meaning "books." It consists of the Old and New Testaments. The Hebrew scriptures making up the Old Testament were created long before Jesus's time. In contrast, the twenty-seven books of the New Testament, which deal primarily with Jesus as the Messiah, his disciples, and other early Jewish and gentile Christians, all postdated Jesus's passing. They were composed between about 70 and 120–150 CE.

More specifically, the first four books of the New Testament—Matthew, Mark, Luke, and John—are often called the keystones or bedrock of that collection of writings. They are also called the four Gospels. Mark was composed first, biblical scholars say, most likely between 70 and 75 CE, about four decades or so after Jesus's death. Matthew and Luke were next, written sometime between 80 and 95; John came between 95 and 100. No one knows who wrote them, and experts think the names in their titles are not those of the actual authors,

> *"The Gospels are not biographies in the modern sense of the word."*[23]
>
> —University of Texas scholar L. Michael White

who likely never actually met Jesus. (However, some scholars think that the author of Mark, on which Matthew and Luke were partly based, may have interviewed one or more people who had met Jesus.) Thus, as University of Texas religious studies scholar L. Michael White points out,

> The Gospels are not biographies in the modern sense of the word. Rather, they are stories told in such a way as to evoke a certain image of Jesus for a particular audience. They're trying to convey a message about Jesus, about his significance to the audience and thus we have to think of them as a kind of preaching, as well as storytelling.[23]

The four Gospels, along with the book of Acts and several letters by Paul and other early Christian leaders, provided the

Christians of the period from circa 70 to 200 or so with most of their key beliefs. At first, these texts were not collected to form a single work, as the New Testament did not yet exist. In addition, dozens of other letters, texts, stories, and collections of sayings about Jesus and his disciples circulated through the Roman Empire during the two centuries that followed.

Eventually, about halfway through the fourth century (the 300s), Christian bishops in various sectors of the Roman world decided that the faith's writings containing its beliefs were too disconnected and disorganized. They felt it was time to begin creating a canon (from the Greek word for "measuring stick"), or overall collection, of those core Christian texts. Over the course of a few decades, a general consensus of the bishops on which texts should be in the canon steadily emerged. The New Testament canon was finally complete by about the year 400. Outside of some minor modifications generated by the process of translating it into other languages, it remains largely the same today. So do the faith's central beliefs that are contained in that pivotal Christian literary work.

CHAPTER THREE

Rules to Live By

Like all religions, Christianity has always featured a number of rules that the faithful are expected to follow whenever possible. A great many were set down in writing at one point or another and appear in various books of the Bible, including both the Old and New Testaments. Other rules developed over time within the original Catholic Church and the numerous and diverse Christian denominations that arose over the centuries beginning with the rise of Protestantism during the 1500s.

The Ten Commandments

Probably the most famous Christian rules—the Ten Commandments—were also the first to be recognized and embraced by the earliest Christians. This is because they were Jews, and the Ten Commandments were an integral part of Jewish lore and religious and social instruction. Those core rules are listed in the Old Testament book of Exodus.

The Exodus, as described in that ancient text, was the flight of the Jews from Egypt, where they had long been enslaved. Having escaped into the deserts of the Sinai Peninsula, they came to Mt. Sinai, where their leader, Moses, received a communication from God. "The Lord called Moses to the top of the mountain," it states in Exodus, "and Moses went up."[24] There, Jews and Christians believe, God delivered the Ten Commandments to Moses, who then introduced them to his people at the base of the mountain.

According to the book of Exodus, Moses led the Jews out of bondage in Egypt. God spoke to Moses and directed him to show a list of rules to his people. These rules were called the Ten Commandments.

The first commandment states that God's chosen people, the Jews, should worship no other gods but him. The second rule also deals with the worship of other deities. It reads,

> You shall not make for yourself a graven [carved] image, or any likeness of anything that is in heaven above, or that is in the earth beneath, or that is in the water under the earth; you shall not bow down to them or serve them; for I the Lord your God am a jealous God, visiting the iniquity [evil] of the fathers upon the children to the third and the fourth generation of those who hate me, but showing steadfast love to thousands of those who love me and keep my commandments.[25]

The other commandments cover a wide range of religious and social behavior. The fourth, for instance, demands that the people always remember and celebrate the Sabbath, or God's weekly holy day. The sixth states that no one should commit murder; the eighth forbids stealing; and the tenth commandment says that it is wrong to covet, or yearn to have, the wife or property of one's neighbor.

Jesus's Rules for Social Life

The Ten Commandments are far from all-inclusive, as religiously or legally based rules go. There is no commandment that says that abusing one's spouse or children is wrong, for instance. Nor is there any prohibition of slavery or rule against the rich and powerful cheating and otherwise abusing the poor and powerless. Likewise, the Ten Commandments do not state whether it is acceptable or unacceptable to get a divorce, have an abortion, or drink too much alcohol. Also missing is any assertion that peace is superior to war.

For Christians, some of those omissions were addressed in a straightforward manner in Jesus's teachings. According to the Gospel writers, during his fairly short period of preaching, Jesus delivered many sermons in which he discussed morality. At the same time, he suggested that certain ideas and behaviors were more just and constructive than others. Right up to the present, devout Christians have seen those suggested behaviors as both logical and sound rules to live by.

Most modern Christians think that the most memorable of Jesus's public orations is the one that later came to be known as the Sermon on the Mount. No one knows exactly when and where it took place. More certain is that it contains many of Jesus's ethical values and is full of suggestions on how people should treat one another—essentially rules to govern social life. In the speech he consistently emphasizes concepts like mercy, forgiveness, love, and especially treating society's poor and downtrodden decently and with respect.

Regarding the latter, the Sermon on the Mount states, "Blessed are the poor in spirit, for theirs is the kingdom of heaven." Also, "blessed are those who are persecuted." Be charitable toward people who are worse off than yourself, therefore, Jesus urged.

"Give to him who begs from you, and do not refuse him who borrows from you." [26] Moreover, if a person does provide charity for someone in need, no fanfare should be made of it; that is, the giver should not seek applause simply for doing what is right. Therefore, "when you give alms [charity], do not let your left hand know what your right hand is doing, so that your alms may be in secret, and your Father [God], who sees in secret, will reward you." [27]

This decent treatment of people in difficult circumstances, Jesus explained, is based on love for one's fellow human beings. That love, he added, should extend even to those one does not like. Thus, he told his listeners, "I say to you, love your enemies and pray for those who persecute you." [28]

"Blessed Are the Peacemakers"

Another way to demonstrate good feelings toward others, Jesus added, was to refrain from critically judging them by one's own standards. After all, the one who judges typically does not appreciate it when others do that to him or her. "Judge not, that you be not judged," [29] he said. Going hand and hand with that, he added, "whatever you want men to do to you, do also to them." [30] (It should be noted that the social rule embodied in these statements was not original to Jesus. Referred to in later ages as the Golden Rule, versions of it appear in the writings of various ancient peoples predating his time.)

Particularly controversial then, and no less so today, was Jesus's conviction that force, violence, and war were not the most ethical ways to deal with evil and injustice. Instead, he said, one should offer one's enemies friendship. If one does so, he suggested, they may well return the favor, and the result might be peaceful relations, which are always more constructive than hostility and war. To illustrate this concept, he stated, "You have heard that it was said [in Leviticus 24:20 in the Old Testament] 'An eye for an eye and a tooth for a tooth.' But I say to you, do not resist one who is evil. But if any one strikes you on the right cheek, turn to him

Christianity, like other faiths, urges its followers to live by certain rules. However, not all Christians interpret those rules in the same way. For instance, some Christian denominations see abortion as a violation of God's laws while others believe that abortion can be a morally acceptable choice.

Moreover, many Christians pick and choose which faith-based rules to follow. While many denominations oppose sex outside of marriage, for instance, premarital sex is nearly universal among Americans, says the research and policy organization Guttmacher Institute. The tendency to follow some rules and not others or to mix and match religious traditions may be on the rise. Baylor University sociologist and researcher Paul K. McClure calls this phenomenon religious "tinkering." Referring to his study, published in December 2017 in the *Journal for the Scientific Study of Religion*, McClure says, "Tinkering means that people feel they're no longer beholden to institutions or religious dogma." He believes that Internet use may be a factor. He explains: "Today, perhaps in part because many of us spend so much time online, we're more likely to understand our religious participation as free agents who can tinker with a plurality of religious ideas—even different, conflicting religions—before we decide how we want to live."

The Internet exposes people to all sorts of ideas, beliefs, and traditions—religious and otherwise. This type of exposure, McClure says, encourages religious tinkering. Given the ubiquity of the Internet, the phenomenon of picking and choosing is likely to grow.

"Using the Internet May Prompt Religious 'Tinkering' Rather than Belief in Only One Religion," Baylor University, January 16, 2018. www.baylor.edu.

the other [cheek] also. And if anyone would sue you and take your coat, let him have your cloak as well."[31] Similarly, in one of his most famous phrases, Jesus asserted, "Blessed are the peacemakers, for they shall be called the sons of God."[32]

The Evolution of the Seven Virtues
These and Jesus's other rules governing people's social interactions did not die with him. His disciples and other followers kept them alive and passed them on to others. Accompanying these

rules were others, many of which came from Jewish ethical tradition. This is not surprising; for a few decades after Jesus's passing, most Christians still thought of themselves as Jews.

This explains why early Christians based some of their initial ideas about ethical behavior on passages from the Hebrew scriptures, or Old Testament. Particularly influential in this respect was a section of the book of Proverbs that tells what a good person should *not* do: "There are six things that the Lord hates, seven that are an abomination to him: haughty eyes, a lying tongue, and hands that shed innocent blood, a heart that devises wicked plans, feet that hurry to run to evil, a lying witness who testifies falsely, and one who sows discord in a family."[33]

Such lists of so-called sins in the scriptures were almost always the basis for contrasting virtuous behaviors that over time came to be labeled Christian virtues. Many of these social rules, some based on Hebrew writings and some based on variations of Jesus's teachings, are listed in passages of the New Testament.

A woman gives food to a homeless man in Germany. Jesus spoke about the virtues of showing kindness and respect to all, and he emphasized the need to be charitable to the poor.

Prominent, for example, are Paul's urgings in the First Epistle to the Corinthians to employ love as often as possible in dealing with life's issues and problems:

> Love is patient; love is kind; love is not envious or boastful or arrogant or rude. It does not insist on its own way; it is not irritable or resentful; it does not rejoice in wrongdoing, but rejoices in the truth. It bears all things, believes all things, hopes all things, endures all things. Love never ends. [And] now faith, hope, and love abide, these three; and the greatest of these is love.[34]

Some more explicit rules for virtuous behavior appear in the Epistle to the Romans: "Live in harmony with one another; do not be haughty, but associate with the lowly; do not claim to be wiser than you are. Do not repay anyone evil for evil, but take thought for what is noble in the sight of all. If it is possible, so far as it depends on you, live peaceably with all."[35]

These and other passages from early Christian writings were later supplemented by statements of moral rules by Augustine and other early and medieval Christian theologians. The result was that the ever-evolving and expanding Catholic Church came to adopt a list of seven moral virtues. Later, after Protestant groups split with Catholicism, many of the new faiths kept those seven rules for ethical behavior (and sometimes added others). These are the seven most commonly listed rules: be generous, be modest or humble, be patient, be kind, be chaste (sexually pure), be temperate (do everything in moderation), and be diligent (hardworking).

"Faith, hope, and love abide, these three; and the greatest of these is love."[34]

—St. Paul

Modern Changes to Older Rules

A great many of the religious and social rules advocated by modern Christian groups derive from or are variations of those traditional seven rules. Some have been adapted or created to address societal changes. Many Christian groups have long

Changing Church Rules Regarding Transgender Folk

"Religious institutions are starting to formally address the participation of transgender people in their congregations," says Pew Research Center statistical scientist Aleksandra Sanstrom. When society first became aware that transgender (trans) people exist, in the early-to-mid twentieth century, little was known about that aspect of human identity. There was an assumption that it was a medical disorder, so Christian groups tended to reject the transition that some people underwent. Since the beginning of the twenty-first century, however, science has shown that a trans person is indeed an individual who identifies as one gender but who was designated a different gender at birth.

Seeing that this is not the trans person's fault or intention, some churches have become more accepting. The Episcopalians, Unitarians, Evangelical Lutherans, American Presbyterians, and members of the United Church of Christ, among others, now say that trans people should be part of church life and allowed to become ministers. "On the other side of the spectrum," Sandstrom states, some Christian churches "do not accept those who change their gender but instead look to provide special pastoral care for transgender people. The Lutheran Church–Missouri Synod, for instance, gives advice to ministers on how to counsel transgender people and encourage them to seek treatment." Meanwhile, in 2014 the Southern Baptist Convention adopted the position that transgender people can only become members "if they repent" what is considered to be a sin or delusion.

Aleksandra Sandstrom, "Religious Groups' Policies on Transgender Members Vary Widely," Pew Research Center, December 2, 2015. www.pewresearch.org.

regarded homosexuality as immoral, for instance. In 1975 the Catholic Church's committee that makes official policies and rules restated a long-standing church position. Homosexuality, it said, is "contrary to the creative wisdom of God." Further, "homosexual relationships jeopardize the rights of traditional (heterosexual, married) families. Some discrimination against gays and lesbians is [therefore] morally permissible and is justified, because of the threat that homosexuals may pose to 'genuine families,' and to 'protect the common good.'"[36] In the same decade the United Methodist Church stated that the "practice of homosexuality is incompatible with Christian teaching."[37] A similar statement came from the Evangelical Lutheran Church of America in 1993. Its bishops agreed that "there is basis neither in Scripture nor tradition for the establishment of an official ceremony by this church for the blessing of a homosexual relationship."[38]

These samples reflect the views of the vast majority of Christian denominations up to and during much of the twentieth century. During that same century, however, scientists across the world studied the phenomenon of homosexuality and eventually concluded that it is not a choice but instead a normal sexual variation that occurs in a minority of people in each new generation. In 1973 the American Psychiatric Association removed homosexuality from its list of mental illnesses. Another definitive scientific statement on the matter came from the American Psychological Association in 1994: "The research on homosexuality is very clear. Homosexuality is neither mental illness nor moral depravity. It is simply the way a minority of our population expresses human love and sexuality."[39]

> *"[The] Practice of homosexuality is incompatible with Christian teaching."[37]*
>
> —A 1970s rule of the United Methodist Church

In the face of hundreds of other studies and statements like these, some Christian groups began to alter their rules on the subject. In 2009, for instance, a task force of the Evangelical Lutheran Church of America stated that the church

> extols the place of family, right relationships, love, Christian values, sexuality, mutuality, commitment, the benefits to society and the church of committed relationships, and the diversity of successful families within church and society. The Proposed Social Statement clearly places same-gender committed relationships among those.[40]

Varying Rules Regarding Divorce

Other Christian rules that have undergone changes in modern times are those dealing with divorce. While marriage is considered a sacred bond by all Christian denominations—and other religions, for that matter—attitudes toward divorce have changed over time. Divorce was roundly frowned on by most Christian denominations for centuries, in large part because of statements about it in both the Old and New Testaments. In Matthew, for example, Jesus says, "What therefore God has joined together, let not man put asunder." He adds, "I say unto you, whosoever shall put away [divorce] his wife, except it be for fornication [having sex with another man], and shall marry another, commits adultery."[41]

Thus, traditional Christian teachings consider marriage to be a lifelong commitment. To this day, a number of the faith's denominations maintain that stance. The Catholic Church, for instance, still forbids divorce, saying that only the death of a spouse can end a marriage. (One exception is a church-granted annulment, a document that says, in effect, that no valid marriage ever occurred.) Despite this church teaching, some Catholics and other Christians whose churches are against divorce simply ignore such rules and get divorced. They may or may not face penalties of various kinds from church officials. A typical penalty for getting divorced is the loss of the right to take Holy Communion (in those churches that practice that ritual).

> **"Divorced persons are permitted by the Church to marry again without the stain of immorality."[43]**
>
> —Modern statement of a Mormon leader

Meanwhile, a number of other Christian groups have altered their rules to permit divorce, either for specific reasons only or, in some cases, *any* reason. Generally, their reasoning for the change has been that the pressures and other realities of modern life make happiness in marriage difficult for some people, who should have a way to rectify that. Addressing the issue head-on in 1980, the Presbyterian Church stated, "The church must deal both with those whose marriages are breaking and with its own role and task. The church is to be a community of healing [and] forgiveness, and it should mediate forgiveness in the brokenness of divorce among its members."[42] In a similar vein, a high-ranking official of the Mormon church states, "In this day, divorces are permitted in accordance with civil statutes, and the divorced persons are permitted by the

Marriage is considered a sacred bond by all Christians. However, attitudes toward divorce have changed over time, and people may not always face a penalty from their church.

Church to marry again without the stain of immorality which under a higher system would attend such a course."[43]

Another example is the position of the US branch of the Greek Orthodox Church. Once extremely rigid in its rules about divorce, it now allows a couple to end their marriage in select cases. An official church document states, "The only church ground for divorce is adultery, but through special mercy the church will make exceptions."[44] Among these exceptions are when one spouse is shown to be insane; when one spouse is in prison for more than seven years; and when one spouse forces the other to take part in illegal activities.

The Realities of Modern Life

The rules and policies of the various Christian denominations cover many other social, political, and spiritual issues and themes. A few of the more talked about ones include the nature of sin; contraception, abortion, and other matters related to sexuality; alcohol consumption and recreational drug use; the importance of attending church on a regular basis; the proper roles and behavior of members of the clergy; and the acceptable treatment of animals.

The rules that the faithful are expected to follow in connection with such issues often differ from one Christian group to another. In part, this is because different denominations have come to deal with the realities and pressures of modern life in distinct ways. Among the most prevalent and powerful of these pressures are the mass media, new technologies, increased social and geographic mobility, and frequently changing moral codes.

As a result of these factors, Oxford University scholar Brian Wilson points out, society is in a state of constant and increasingly swift flux. In that situation, he says, older rules sometimes come to be reinterpreted or even abandoned. The Christian community as a whole, he predicts, is destined to undergo "further change and perhaps more rapid change than has been evident even in the very recent past."[45] Therefore, Wilson concludes, the social policies and various other rules of at least some Christian groups are likely to continue to change with the times.

CHAPTER FOUR

How Do Christians Practice Their Faith?

Christianity has a long and rich tradition of diverse ceremonies and other practices. Some of them vary considerably from one denomination to another. For instance, a number of churches follow the example of the Catholic mass and conduct elaborate weekly ceremonies featuring clergy donning traditional costumes (called vestments), displays of sacred objects, spoken recitations of traditional verses, the use of incense, music, and more. Other denominations have simpler public ceremonies. One of the simplest of all is the so-called Quaker meeting; during this ceremony, a few believers sit together in silence, which is broken only when one member decides to tell the others what is on his or her mind.

Nevertheless, there are several common or similar practices, versions of which can be found in most Christian denominations. They include a Sunday worship service; prayer, said either aloud by a group (called corporate prayer) or privately by an individual; enacting ancient rituals like baptism, confirmation, confession, and communion; studies and readings of the Bible; and taking part in charitable giving in the name of God and one's church.

Early Christian Rituals

Many of these rituals and other practices derive from versions begun by the small Christian communities that existed during the faith's first two or three centuries. In those days communal worship led by a clergyman, either a bishop or some other leader, took place on Sunday. That tradition was based on the belief that Jesus's resurrection had occurred on a Sunday. There were also worship services held on Wednesdays and Fridays. The early

Christians viewed those two days as times of sadness because, it was thought, Jesus's disciple Judas had betrayed him to the authorities in Jerusalem on those days.

The early Sunday worship services took place in private homes since formal churches did not yet exist. The worshippers met in a house's biggest room, which had a table on one end and, when possible, stools or chairs filling most of the chamber. The bishop or other person in charge sat behind the table, and the worshippers, who made up the local congregation, sat on the stools and chairs. At first, free men, free women, and slaves of both genders were segregated into separate sections.

The rituals that took place in these early Christian communal gatherings appear to have included simple or basic versions of practices that endured over time and still exist in more formal settings and versions. Among them were hymn singing, praying, and reading from the cherished texts that eventually became formalized in the New Testament. (In those early centuries there were no printed copies of the texts, so the bishop or other leader read a handwritten copy aloud to the worshippers.)

The Ceremony of the Eucharist

Another key element of early Christian worship, which has survived to the present almost unchanged, was the Eucharist, from a Greek word meaning "thanksgiving." This ceremony, practiced today by most of the faith's denominations, is better known as Holy Communion. In the original Christian services, the worshippers each ate a small piece of bread, which represented Jesus's body. They also sipped some wine, which stood for his blood.

Accompanying the Eucharistic actions was a prayer in which the bishop or other leader and worshippers interacted. He said, "God be with you," and they answered in unison, "And with your spirit." Then he stated, "We give thanks, O God, through your beloved son Jesus Christ." The leader went on to quote Jesus, who during the famous Last Supper with his disciples said, "Take, eat [this bread that] is my body which is broken for you," and "this [wine] is my blood which is shed for you. When you do this, do it in remembrance of me."[46]

Today most Christians—including Catholics, Anglicans, Lutherans, Methodists, Eastern Orthodox, and numerous others—

The customs of the Catholic mass reflect the Church's strict adherence to tradition and ceremony. Some formal masses include the burning of incense, donning of traditional vestments, and singing by choirs.

take part in the Eucharist. Some of these groups substitute a small, thin wafer for the bread representing Jesus's body. Groups that frown on drinking alcoholic beverages—for instance, most Methodists—use grape juice instead of wine.

Catholics and members of some other denominations believe that during the Eucharist ceremony the bread and wine actually transform into Jesus's flesh and blood. This mystical process is known as transubstantiation. Despite whether they accept the reality of that transformation, virtually all Christians who take part in the Eucharist believe that the ceremony draws them closer to Jesus and confirms their faith in him.

The Mass and Other Christian Services

In addition to the Eucharist, modern Christian worship services include a wide range of activities and other features. Among the more elaborate services is the Catholic mass. There is the average Sunday mass and a few more elaborate versions—called High Masses—that take place on special feast days, including Easter.

The Eucharist is a ritual practiced by many Christian denominations. The ceremony involves consuming a wafer and wine that represent the body and blood of Christ.

A typical mass includes the reading of passages from the Bible. The first one usually comes from the Old Testament and the second from the New Testament. These excerpts tend to vary from one service to another. After the readings, the congregation stands and recites the Nicene Creed, a list of core beliefs that early Christian leaders introduced during the 300s CE. It states, in part, that the worshippers believe in God, who created the universe, and his son, Jesus Christ. "For our salvation," it goes on,

he came down from heaven, was made flesh from the Holy Spirit and Mary the virgin and became man. He was crucified for us under [the Roman official] Pontius Pilate, suffered, and was buried. He rose again on the third day, according to the Scriptures, and ascended into the heavens. He sits on the right hand of the Father and will come again with glory to judge the living and the dead. His kingdom will not end. [We] look forward to the resurrection of the dead and in the life in the age to come. Amen.[47]

This statement of belief is used in similar fashion in many other Christian denominations, including the Eastern Orthodox, Anglican, Lutheran, and Methodist Churches, to name only a few.

After these sorts of preliminaries, the priest in the Catholic mass, or the minister or pastor in most Protestant denominations, prepares for the Eucharist, after which the members of the congregation file up toward the altar to receive the bread and wine. After the Eucharist is finished, the Catholic priest blesses the worshippers and dismisses them. In many Protestant denominations, the parishioners sing hymns in unison after the Eucharist as well as at various other points during an average service.

> *"He rose again on the third day, according to the Scriptures, and ascended into the heavens."*[47]
>
> —The Nicene Creed on Jesus's resurrection

The Ritual of Baptism

The Eucharist occupies a central position in most Christian worship services. It is one of a number of major Christian practices that some denominations call sacraments and others ordinances. Whatever people call them, these central rituals are seen as ways to bring a believer closer to Jesus and to his or her individual church or ministry. Such rites also serve the function of teaching followers about a denomination's various beliefs and why they are important.

The number of sacraments or ordinances differs from one Christian group to another. Catholics and Eastern Orthodox believers, for instance, recognize seven sacraments, counting the

Eucharist. The other six are baptism, confirmation, penance (or confession), anointing sick people, matrimony (or marriage), and holy orders (joining the priesthood). By contrast, Lutherans and Presbyterians recognize just three sacraments—the Eucharist, baptism, and confession. Anglicans, Methodists, and some other denominations accept only the Eucharist and baptism as sacraments yet still take part in the others as lesser rituals. Baptists, Pentecostals, and Mormons call such practices ordinances. A few Christian groups, including the Quakers, are nonsacramental, meaning they recognize none of these rituals.

Next to the Eucharist, baptism is the most widespread and revered of the commonly practiced sacraments or ordinances. All Christians who accept baptism see it as a major form of initiation into one's church or ministry. By either being immersed in or sprinkled with water, the person undergoes a symbolic transformation. His or her former self is in a sense washed away and a new self emerges, one reborn in Jesus Christ's grace. According to the noted historian of Christianity Justo L. Gonzalez, typically this sacrament was administered on Easter Sunday. Gonzalez explains that

> early in the third century it was customary for those about to be baptized to fast on Friday and Saturday, and to be baptized very early Sunday morning, which was the time of the resurrection of Jesus. The candidates were completely naked, the men separated from the women. On emerging from the waters, the neophytes [initiates] were given white robes, as a sign of their new life in Christ. They were also given water to drink, as a sign that they were thoroughly cleansed, both outside and inside.[48]

Spiritual Power in the Sacraments

Among the Christian sacraments, the Eucharist and baptism are arguably the most widely cherished and practiced. Here, scholar Maurice Wiles suggests how practicing them might make worshippers feel closer to Jesus.

> The fundamental meaning and structure of the two sacraments is essentially the same. Each ties together the realms of creation, redemption, and transformation, and makes them effective in the life of the believer. A sacrament by definition embodies a positive evaluation of the created order. It uses some aspect of the physical world in a manner designed to convey a religious meaning and a spiritual power. Both baptism and Eucharist recall in action the death of Christ and make it effective in the life of the participating worshiper. How past history, present experience, and eternal meaning are brought together in the sacramental action has been variously understood. The competing understandings have often been in violent opposition to one another—and sometimes still are. But at the heart of the most contradictory theorizing is a common conviction. [It is] that in the Eucharist the eternal love of God, decisively expressed in the crucifixion and resurrection of Jesus, is brought into special and transforming relation with the lives of the believing worshipers.

Maurice Wiles, "What Christians Believe," in *The Oxford History of Christianity*, ed. John McManners. New York: Oxford University Press, 2001, p. 581.

Today the vast majority of Christian denominations baptize their members in one of two ways. One is infant baptism and the other is the baptism of adults, most commonly labeled believer baptism. The baptizing of babies is based largely on the notion that God prepares people for faith in him before they know what may happen to them in the future. Those who practice this form of baptism say it is a blessing to bring unknowing infants into God's grace as soon as possible following birth. In the act itself, usually the priest or minister sprinkles some water on the baby's forehead.

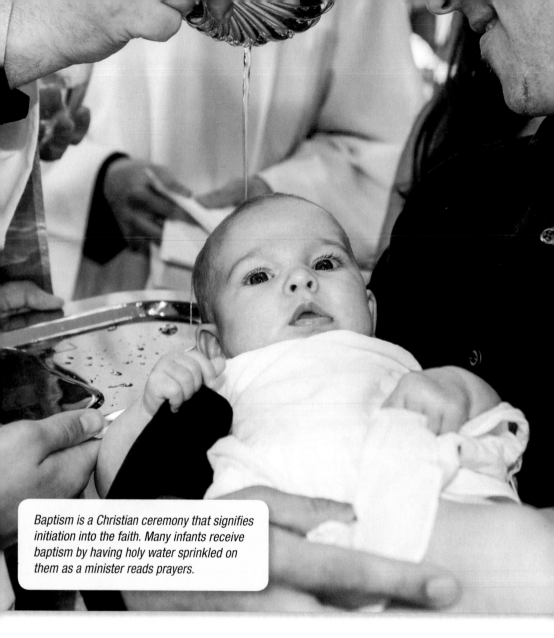

Baptism is a Christian ceremony that signifies initiation into the faith. Many infants receive baptism by having holy water sprinkled on them as a minister reads prayers.

In comparison, those who practice believer baptism—for instance, Baptists and many other fundamentalist Christians—feel that this ritual should be based only on the faith of the believer. Since he or she can gain that faith only knowingly, over a period of years, a person must be older when baptism occurs. That also ensures that the initiate can assent to take part in the ritual. The chief method of believer baptism is total immersion in water. An official statement of the American Baptist Church declares, "We insist that baptism be administered only to those who have the maturity to understand its profound significance: resurrection to new life in Christ. And we follow the biblical example set by Christ when we fully immerse in water, a beautiful symbolic statement of that new life.[49]

Other Sacraments

Another important sacrament, confirmation, is seen by Catholics, Eastern Orthodox believers, and some other Christians as a later affirmation of the religious initiation that began with baptism. That is, the person, most often in his or her teens and after taking some religious classes, is confirmed to be a member of the congregation and a believer in Jesus Christ. In the confirmation ceremony, a member of the clergy applies some holy oil to the initiate's forehead, usually while the latter's relatives and friends look on.

Of the other Christian practices considered to be sacraments or ordinances, two of the more widely observed are often called the healing sacraments. One is confession, in which a believer confides a personal act of wrongdoing to either a member of the clergy or a group of fellow believers. That wrongdoing may consist of a small misstep—for example, a casual lie—or a serious sin, such as stealing or adultery. Whatever the offense might be, the person seeks forgiveness for it. Usually he or she agrees to do some form of penance for it that will satisfy God and thereby heal the wrongdoer.

> *"We insist that baptism be administered only to those who have the maturity to understand its profound significance."*[49]
>
> —Officials of the American Baptist Church

The other healing sacrament, anointing the sick, is based directly on the biblical tales in which Jesus and his disciples aided people afflicted with various infirmities. In the Gospel of Mark, Jesus states that those who believe in him "will lay their hands on the sick, and they will recover."[50] To most Christians, this passage inspires two sorts of help for sick people. In one, a priest, minister, or other member of the clergy tries to heal a person.

The oldest and most basic Christian prayer is the Our Father, also called the Lord's Prayer, spoken by Jesus in the famous Sermon on the Mount. It is the prayer that inspired or affected, to one degree or another, the development of all subsequent Christian prayers. It was not the only prayer that Jesus said, however, as evidenced by numerous passages in the New Testament. These episodes have also inspired generations of Christians. The actual words of most of Jesus's prayers are not mentioned in the Bible. In Matthew, for example, after leaving a crowd of followers, he "went up into the hills by himself to pray." In fact, many of the times that Jesus prays in the New Testament he goes far away from other people, apparently not wanting to be disturbed. This happens in Mark: "In the morning, a great while before day, he arose and went out to a lonely place, and there he prayed." Similarly, in Luke, "In these days he went out into the hills to pray, and all night he continued in prayer to God." These passages suggest that prayer was often a very private act for Jesus.

Matthew 14:23; Mark 1:35; Luke 6:12.

In the other, individual Christians are urged to do whatever they can for the ill persons among them, including taking care of sick family members and praying for those who suffer from disease and other ailments.

The Tradition of Prayer

In addition to worship services and the practices surrounding the sacraments and ordinances, Christians regularly engage in a number of other rituals. Of these, prayer is by far the most frequent and universal. Christians pray singly in private, as well as in public in groups, as in the case of corporate prayers during church services.

Some prayers are personal and spontaneous and contain ideas and phrases unique to the person praying. Others are traditional and are recognized and repeated by the members of various congregations and denominations. The most famous traditional Christian prayer is the Our Father, or the Lord's Prayer. It has been called the fundamental Christian prayer because it was the one that Jesus recited word for word during the Sermon on the Mount. Virtually all Christian denominations use one or another version of it. The wording of the prayer in Matthew differs somewhat from the version in Luke. Also, over the centuries various Christian groups added or subtracted a few words. The version in Matthew, however, remains the most accepted among the faithful worldwide. That version reads,

> Our Father which art in heaven, hallowed be your name. Your kingdom come. Your will be done in earth, as it is in heaven. Give us this day our daily bread. And forgive us our debts, as we forgive our debtors. And lead us not into temptation, but deliver us from evil. For yours is the kingdom, and the power, and the glory, forever. Amen.[51]

This short but powerful statement provided a framework for all the individual and corporate Christian prayers that followed, right up to the present. First, because Jesus is reported to have said it himself, when a believer repeats it he or she feels a meaningful connection with him. Also, any prayer offered by a believer is presented in Jesus's name. As the Protestant reformer Martin Luther advocated, any Christian prayer should

> *"Forgive us our debts, as we forgive our debtors."[51]*
>
> —From Jesus's Our Father prayer

begin with an expression of praise for God and thanks for his great gifts to humankind. After that opening declaration, the typical prayer consists of an appeal to God to help a person or persons; or show him, her, or them mercy; or keep him, her, or them safe. Although some people do pray for their own enrichment, leaders of all denominations agree that God does not respond to selfish prayers.

From Bell Ringing to Relics

Other practices that are common among many Christian groups create a colorful, at times mystical, atmosphere for believers to meet and worship in. Among them are the use of objects or substances such as candles and incense, the rising smoke from which symbolizes people's prayers floating up to heaven; holy water for baptisms and other ceremonies; ringing bells to mark the times of church services; wearing crucifixes or crosses to show one's commitment to the faith; stained glass windows and paintings that depict scenes from biblical stories; and holy relics, objects that once belonged to saints or other pious individuals and are seen as holy.

These traditional practices, most of which originated during the faith's early centuries, continue to inspire worshippers around the world. As one observer remarks, they provide "21st century believers a tangible, physical connection to the origins of their deeply held faith."[52]

CHAPTER FIVE

What Challenges Does Christianity Face in the Modern World?

Christianity has faced serious challenges since its inception in the first century CE. Among the biggest ones were those that rocked the faith during the Renaissance. During the 1500s the Catholic Church—at that point still the only Christian denomination—was hit by the charge that it had become corrupt. The church's refusal to accept that fact led German theology professor Martin Luther, and later other Christian reformers, to break away and form the first Protestant denominations. Over time many more denominations developed. By 1900 there were at least sixteen hundred distinct Christian denominations; today, only a little more than a century later, the number approaches forty thousand.

On the one hand, the creation of the many Christian denominations breathed new life into the faith as a whole. On the other, it contributed to an altered dynamic—in particular, a lack of unity among Christians. This dynamic has continued right up to the present. Although all Christians follow the same faith, they do not necessarily share a worldview. Some modern Christians believe that abortion and same-sex marriage, for instance, violate the teachings of their faith and should not be allowed. Others do not see a conflict between these actions and their faith and believe that both are choices better left to individuals.

Differing worldviews aside, Christians of all denominations do face some common challenges. One of these challenges involves the need to stay relevant to the questions and concerns of

the modern world. In the eyes of many Americans, faith and the teachings of those religions have become increasingly less relevant in recent times. Indeed, people in the United States today, including Christians, are turning less and less to organized religion as a way to understand and evaluate the events and choices that shape their lives.

Growing Numbers of Unaffiliated Americans

This change has been occurring over nearly three decades. For example, in 1991 only 6 percent of Americans said they had no specific religious affiliation. By 2000 that proportion had risen to 14 percent; by 2012 it was 20 percent; and a mere six years later, in 2018, it reached 25 percent, or a quarter of all Americans. This group, the members of which claim no formal religious identity, is now larger than any single religious group in the United States.

In 2017 the Public Religion Research Institute (PRRI), which compiles statistics on religion, found that in twenty US states the number of religiously unaffiliated residents exceeded the number of people who identify with a particular faith. That includes all Christian denominations in those states. More than four in ten residents of Vermont, for instance, say they do not belong to either a Christian or other religious organization. The same is true for about one-third of the residents of New Hampshire, Oregon, Washington, Colorado, and Hawaii.

The PRRI also found that roughly one-third of all those religiously unaffiliated Americans, most of whom grew up in Christian families, are younger than thirty years old. In contrast, the majority of devout Catholics and Protestants tend to be much older—aged fifty-five on average. In comparison, four decades earlier, in 1976, forty was the average age of American Catholics and forty-five for Protestants. Moreover, at that time most members of Christian families who were under thirty stayed in the faith as they grew older. Seen as a whole, these figures paint a picture of Christianity appealing predominantly to older folk while younger generations turn away from organized churches and congregations. These rapid changes are a major concern for and challenge to Christianity, which has long been the dominant faith in America.

A Lost Belief in Church Teachings

The natural question is why so many Americans have turned away from Christianity—and, to a degree, other faiths—in recent decades. One reason for this phenomenon, as told to researchers from the PRRI, the Pew Research Center, and

Until recently, the United States was an overwhelmingly white Christian country. White Protestants alone made up a clear cultural majority, explain Daniel Cox and Robert P. Jones of the Public Religion Research Institute. They provide some revealing figures that show how that is no longer the case:

> In 1976, roughly eight in ten (81%) Americans identified as white and identified with a Christian denomination. At that time, a majority (55%) of Americans were white Protestants. Much of the decline has occurred in the last few decades. As recently as 1996, white Christians still made up nearly two-thirds (65%) of the public. By 2006, that number dropped to 54%, but white Christians still constituted a majority. But over the last decade, the proportion of white Christians in the U.S. has slipped below majority. Today, only 43% of Americans identify as white and Christian—and only 30% as white and Protestant. Although white Christians have experienced substantial losses nationally, there are notable differences in the sizes of the white Christian populations by state. Today, the states with the highest concentrations of white Christians are generally found in the Midwest and Appalachia, including North Dakota (71%), South Dakota (68%), Iowa (64%), [and] West Virginia (61%). . . . Conversely, white Christians are least plentiful in Hawaii (20%), California (24%), [and] New York (30%). . . . In total, fewer than half (23) of all 50 states have majority white Christian populations.

Daniel Cox and Robert P. Jones, "America's Changing Religious Identity," Public Religion Research Institute, September 6, 2017. www.prri.org.

other groups that do comprehensive studies in this area, is a lack of belief. More specifically, fully 60 percent of those polled said they stopped believing in the teachings of their churches/faiths.

Those polled gave varied reasons to explain why their belief in their faith had waned. Some said that when they were growing up their family was generally not very religious—or at least the parents rarely practiced the faith—and that made the children lose interest in going to church.

Another reason cited by as many as a third of interviewees for why they had turned away from organized Christianity involved gender and sexuality issues. Most often mentioned was what the interviewees considered poor and unfair treatment of members of the LGBT community—that is, lesbian, gay, bisexual, and transgender individuals—by many churches. Some of those who cited this reason were not themselves part of this community. Rather, they were relatives, friends, and coworkers of LGBT members. These LGBT supporters said they were appalled at what they saw as the faith's often negative, uninformed, and unnecessarily hurtful teachings on the issue. As the PRRI's Robert P. Jones and his colleagues report, "Young adults (age 18 to 29) who left their childhood religion are about three times more likely than seniors (age 65 and older) to say negative religious teachings about and treatment of the gay and lesbian community was a primary reason for leaving their childhood faith."[53]

At the same time, members of the LGBT community themselves, who make up possibly 15 to 20 percent of the general population, were also less likely to stay in the faith. According to Jones and his PRRI colleague Daniel Cox,

> *"LGBT Americans are far less likely to identify with any religious group than the public as a whole."*[54]
>
> —Researchers Daniel Cox and Robert P. Jones

LGBT Americans are far less likely to identify with any religious group than the public as a whole. Nearly half (46%) of Americans who identify as lesbian, gay, bisexual, or transgender (LGBT) are religiously unaffiliated. Fewer identify as Christian. Only six percent of LGBT Americans are white evangelical Protestant, while similar numbers identify as white mainline Protestant (8%) and white Catholic (6%). Fewer than one in ten identify as black Protestant (6%), Hispanic Catholic (5%), or Hispanic Protestant (3%).[54]

American Christians told interviewers other reasons for why they had become religiously unaffiliated. For example, about

Today, many younger Christians resist characterizing homosexuality and same-sex marriage as sinful. They often view the faith's negative teachings on members of the LGBT community as hurtful.

one-fifth of Catholics, who compose the biggest subdivision of American Christians, said they largely turned their backs on the church in reaction to the clergy sexual abuse scandal that first made headlines during the late 1980s. As one formerly devout American Catholic puts it, "When we hear day after day the ever more lurid details of priests raping and molesting the children the faithful have entrusted to them, we are horrified, repulsed and heartbroken." She adds, "They [the offending priests] don't follow the rules of the Church. Why should we?"[55]

Trauma and the Source of Morality

A similar proportion of Christians in general said they felt that churches had become so focused on politics that they neglected spiritual matters. Another common reason for losing interest in Christianity, according to the studies, was suffering from some sort of major traumatic event in one's life. Psychiatrist Judith Herman, the author of *Trauma and Recovery*, explains:

> In situations of terror, people spontaneously seek their first source of comfort and protection. Wounded soldiers and raped women cry for their mothers, or for God. When this cry is not answered, the sense of basic trust is shattered. Traumatized people feel utterly abandoned, utterly alone, cast out of the human and divine systems of care and protection that sustain life.[56]

Still another motive for the loss of interest in Christianity (and some other religions) in recent decades involves ethics and morality. Surveys show that there is the perception among a growing number of Americans that a sense of morality can exist outside religion's traditional framework. In prior generations, the vast majority of people, especially Christians, accepted the notion that organized religion was the primary source, even the *only* source, of human morality. In this view, a person could not develop a true set of ethical standards without belief in God and involvement in a God-based faith. That opinion is still widespread among very devout Christians, including about four-fifths of American Catholics.

However, this traditional viewpoint is swiftly changing within the general population. According to Gregory A. Smith of the Pew Research Center, 56 percent of US adults now assert that they can

> *"Raped women cry for their mothers, or for God. When this cry is not answered, the sense of basic trust is shattered."*[56]
>
> —Judith Herman, author of *Trauma and Recovery*

61

be moral and have good values without believing in God. Smith goes on:

> Surveys have long shown that religious "nones," those who describe themselves religiously as atheist, agnostic or "nothing in particular," are more likely than those who identify with a religion to say that belief in God is not a prerequisite for good values and morality. So the public's increased rejection of the idea that belief in God is necessary for morality is due, in large part, to the spike in the share of Americans who are religious "nones." Indeed, the growth in share of Americans who say belief in God is unnecessary for morality tracks closely with the growth in the share of the population that is religiously unaffiliated.[57]

Smith's conclusions are solidly documented by numerous recent surveys and studies. A 2011 Pew Research Center study, for example, found that religious "nones"—those who checked "none" on a survey in answer to what religion they were—made up about 18 percent of the country's population. By 2017, the surveys showed, the share of unaffiliated Americans had risen to 25 percent. Also, roughly two-thirds of unaffiliated Americans now hold that children can learn good values without being brought up in a religious faith.

Searching for Solutions

Whatever the reasons may be for the continuing drain of believers from their ranks, many Christians are worried about that trend and would like to reverse it. Those who most often turn their backs on the churches are younger Christians, including millennials (people born between the mid-1980s and mid-1990s) and members of Generation Z (born between the mid-1990s and up to about 2012). Interestingly, members of those two generations who remain believers are in the forefront of the Christians who have avidly been searching for solutions to the problem.

Overall, their most prevalent approach to luring lost youth back into the faith is a sort of hands-on activism. Simply showing up at church each Sunday, worshipping there, and then going home is no longer enough, says Shawn Williams, pastor of the Commu-

Psychiatrists, grief counselors, and other experts on the human mind and how it works point out that various kinds of trauma can seriously damage a person's confidence, emotional stability, or even his or her religious faith. "Our faith has been built over time as we live and construct in our minds the things we believe in," says Hawaii-based educator and trauma counselor Victoria McGee. "Trauma can shatter those beliefs in an instant." She goes on,

> Faith is a product of the spirit. Faith is the abstract knowing that the Divine is constant. When there is a crack in that knowing, what can heal it? When there is a tear in the fabric of faith, what will mend it? After 9/11 there was a wonderful quote by Mr. Rogers going around. His advice in times of extreme trauma was to "Look for the helpers." This is a start in restoring our faith. If you have survived a trauma, you were likely helped, if not immediately after, then soon after. Look at those helpers. For me it was kind police officers, a calm and soft-voiced trauma nurse, and my friends who came in the middle of the night without asking why I needed them, they just came. When I looked back on all that, it made a few stitches in my torn faith. I could trust the goodness of those people, and they had faith in me that I would survive this. It was a start.

Victoria McGee, "Trauma and Restoring Faith," *Huffington Post*, December 6, 2017. www.huffingtonpost.com.

nity Christian Church in Naperville, Illinois. Millennials, who make up a hefty proportion of his congregation, he says, do not

> want to sit on the sidelines and observe. If they're going to be part of a church, it must have value and meaning. In generations like the Boomers [born between the late 1940s and early 1960s], people attend church out of some moral obligation to do so. Millennials won't have any of that. If it doesn't provide meaning and value to them, they won't participate. They'll go and find something that does have meaning and value.[58]

For many of these young Christians, the meaning and value they seek comes from getting involved in political, social, and/or scientific activities outside the church. They then share their outside experiences with their fellow worshippers and share their religious faith with the people they meet outside of church. The hope is that this cross-over approach will bring at least some of those who lack faith into the ranks of the church.

Taking a Stand Through Faith

Nebraska native Matthew Maly is an example of an earnest millennial Christian who has embraced this activist approach. He notes that nearly 70 percent of white conservative Protestants in Nebraska support the death penalty. Maly is among the minority of local white Protestants who are against the death penalty. But instead of keeping that controversial social-political viewpoint to himself, he actively shares it with others.

Maly explains that reading the biblical passages in which Jesus condemns violence and killing is what inspired him to reject the death penalty. Thus, it was an important element of his faith that led him to seek social justice outside the church. He often appeals to his fellow conservative Christians by pointing out that executing criminals is not only against Jesus's teachings but also is unnecessarily expensive. Nebraska spends about $14 million a year to maintain the death penalty, he points out. It is far cheaper, he adds, to sentence criminals to life in prison without parole.

Maly devotes much of his time to delivering lectures on the death penalty issue both inside and outside the church. He also invites former death row inmates whose sentences were overturned to give talks in schools and churches. In addition, he urges pastors to speak about the death penalty to their congregations. "A lot of people will change their minds based on what they hear from the pulpit,"[59] he says.

By getting his fellow parishioners to take a stand on a controversial issue, Maly hopes to make the church more interesting and attractive to local millennials and others who feel that as an institution the church is outmoded. If the church seems active and relevant within the greater community, he feels, it will attract more adherents. Similar activism launched by young Christians is ongoing across the United States. Typical issues that are helping to transform churches with large proportions of young people include climate change, racial inequality, and safety and justice for immigrants and international refugees.

Some young Christians find meaning in their faith by getting involved in social issues that are important to them. Some take on an activist approach and share their views with people they meet outside of the church.

There is no way to know whether this approach, along with others, will eventually reverse the present trend of young people leaving Christian churches. Indeed, no one knows for sure what Christianity's future will be and whether it will continue to be relevant within society. But in trying to predict the faith's future, it might be instructive to look at its past. Over the course of close to twenty centuries Christianity has met and ultimately overcome innumerable challenges, large and small. In the eyes of history, at least, there is every reason to believe that the world's biggest faith will find ways to continue to survive and prosper.

SOURCE NOTES

Introduction: Christianity's Eternal Mission

1. Quoted in Vatican News, "Pope Francis Greets Cardinals: Full Text." www.news.va.
2. Pope Francis, "Homily of the Holy Father Pope Francis, March 14, 2013," Holy See. http://w2.vatican.va.
3. Colossians 1:6, 4:3–4.
4. Quoted in Goodreads, "Quotes About Evangelism." www.goodreads.com.

Chapter One: The Origins of Christianity

5. Michael Grant, *History of Rome*. New York: Scribner's, 2005, p. 342.
6. Apuleius, *The Golden Ass*, trans. P.G. Walsh. New York: Oxford University Press, 1995, p. 224.
7. Charles Freeman, *Egypt, Greece, and Rome*. New York: Oxford University Press, 1996, p. 490.
8. Matthew 5:5–6.
9. Acts 9:3–6.
10. Ignatius of Antioch, "Letter to the Smyrnaeans," Early Christian Writings. www.earlychristianwritings.com.
11. Tacitus, *The Annals of Imperial Rome*, trans. Michael Grant. New York: Penguin, 1989, p. 365; and see Paul Brians, "Tacitus: Nero's Persecution of the Christians," Washington State University. https://brians.wsu.edu.
12. Harold Mattingly, *The Man in the Roman Street*. New York: Norton, 1966, p. 56.
13. Quoted in Eusebius, *Ecclesiastical History*, vol. 1, trans. Roy J. Deferrari. Washington, DC: Catholic University of America Press, 1955, p. 269.

Chapter Two: What Do Christians Believe?

14. Quoted in Creeds of Christendom, "Hippolytus's Account of the Baptismal Service." www.creeds.net.
15. Tertullian, *Against Praxeas*, trans. Peter Holms, New Advent. www.newadvent.org.

16. Helen Keeler and Susan Grimbly, *The Everything Catholicism Book*. Avon, MA: Adams Media, p. 65.
17. Maurice Wiles, "What Christians Believe," in *The Oxford History of Christianity*, ed. John McManners. New York: Oxford University Press, 2001, pp. 578–79.
18. Mark 16:5–7.
19. John 21:12–14.
20. First Corinthians 15:12–13.
21. Quoted in Religious Tolerance, "Salvation and the Presbyterian Church." www.religioustolerance.org.
22. Augustine, *The City of God*, in *Works of Augustine*, trans. Marcus Dods. Chicago: Encyclopaedia Britannica, 1952, p. 618.
23. Quoted in *Frontline*, "What Are the Gospels?," PBS. www.pbs.org.

Chapter Three: Rules to Live By

24. Exodus 19:20.
25. Exodus 20:4.
26. Matthew 5:3, 10, 42.
27. Matthew 6:3–4.
28. Matthew 5:44.
29. Matthew 7:1.
30. Matthew 7:12
31. Matthew 5:38–40.
32. Matthew 5:9.
33. Proverbs 6:16–19.
34. First Corinthians 13:4–8, 13.
35. Romans 12:16–18.
36. Quoted in Religious Tolerance, "The Roman Catholic Church and Homosexuality: Statements and Events Prior to 1997." www.religioustolerance.org.
37. Quoted in Religious Tolerance, "The United Methodist Church and Homosexuality." www.religioustolerance.org.
38. Quoted in Religious Tolerance, "Evangelical Lutheran Church of America: Events from 1974 to 1999." www.religioustolerance.org.
39. Quoted in TeachtheFacts.org, "What the Professional Organizations Say." www.teachthefacts.org.

40. Quoted in Religious Tolerance, "Evangelical Lutheran Church of America: Events About the Social Statements Prior to the 2009 Church-wide Assembly." www.religioustolerance.org.
41. Matthew 19:6–9.
42. Quoted in Religious Tolerance, "Divorce and Remarriage: Statements by Christian Denominations." www.religioustolerance.org.
43. Quoted in Religious Tolerance, "Divorce and Remarriage."
44. Quoted in Religious Tolerance, "Divorce and Remarriage."
45. Bryan Wilson, "New Images of Christian Community," in McManners, *The Oxford History of Christianity*, p. 617.

Chapter Four: How Do Christians Practice Their Faith?

46. Quoted in Brian Moynahan, *The Faith: A History of Christianity*. New York: Doubleday, 2002, p. 56.
47. Quoted in Tony Lane, *Exploring Christian Thought*. Nashville: Thomas Nelson, 1996, p. 35.
48. Justo L. Gonzalez, *The Story of Christianity*, vol. 1, *The Early Church to the Dawn of the Reformation*. San Francisco: Harper and Row, 2010, p. 96.
49. American Baptist Churches USA, "The Bible." www.abc-usa.org.
50. Mark 16:13.
51. Matthew 6:9–13.
52. Drew Kann, "The Mystery and Controversy of Christian Relics," CNN, April 18, 2017. www.cnn.com.

Chapter Five: What Challenges Does Christianity Face in the Modern World?

53. Robert P. Jones et al., "Exodus: Why Americans are Leaving Religion—and Why They're Unlikely to Come Back," Public Religion Research Institute, September 22, 2016. www.prri.org.
54. Daniel Cox and Robert P. Jones, "America's Changing Religious Identity," Public Religion Research Institute, September 6, 2017. www.prri.org.

55. Michele Langevine Leiby, "Losing My Religion: One Catholic's Crisis of Faith," *Huffington Post*, May 25, 2011. www.huffing tonpost.com.

56. Quoted in Victoria McGee, "Trauma and Restoring Faith," *Huffington Post*, December 6, 2017. www.huffingtonpost .com.

57. Gregory A. Smith, "A Growing Share of Americans Say It's Not Necessary to Believe in God to Be Moral," Pew Research Center, October 16, 2017. www.pewresearch.org.

58. Quoted in Marian V. Liautaud, "5 Things That Millennials Wish the Church Would Be," Exponential. https://exponential.org.

59. Quoted in Serena Solomon, "Meet the Woke Young People Trying to Make Christianity Cool Again," *Vice*, November 3, 2017. www.vice.com.

FOR FURTHER RESEARCH

Books

Dennis J. Driscoll, *Rome, Europe, and the World: A Reader's Guide to the Catholic Church*. Charleston, SC: Amazon Digital Services, 2017.

Adolph Fehlauer, *The Life and Faith of Martin Luther*. Charleston, SC: Amazon Digital Services, 2016.

Peter Martin, *Explore the Bible Book by Book*. Oxford, UK: Lion Children's, 2017.

Ron Rhodes, *The Complete Guide to Christian Denominations: Understanding the History, Beliefs, and Differences*. Eugene, OR: Harvest House, 2015.

Kelly Roscoe, *The Fall of the Roman World and the Rise of Christianity*. Brooklyn, NY: Britannica Educational, 2017.

Danielle Watson, *The Church in Medieval Europe*. New York: Cavendish Square, 2016.

Internet Sources

Becka A. Alper, "5 Facts About Israeli Christians," Pew Research Center, May 10, 2016. www.pewresearch.org/fact-tank/2016/05/10/5-facts-about-israeli-christians.

Paul Brians, "Tacitus: Nero's Persecution of the Christians," Washington State University. https://brians.wsu.edu/2016/11/14/tacitus-neros-persectution-of-the-christians.

Mary Fairchild, "How Many Christians Are in the World Today?," ThoughtCo, December 19, 2017. https://www.thoughtco.com/christianity-statistics-700533.

Frontline, "What Are the Gospels?," PBS. www.pbs.org/wgbh/pages/frontline/shows/religion/story/gospels.html.

History Channel, "Christianity," www.history.com/topics/history-of-christianity.

Felix Just, "Virtue and Vice Lists in the Bible," Catholic Resources for Bible, Liturgy, Art, and Theology. http://catholic-resources.org/Bible/Epistles-VirtuesVices.htm.

ReligionFacts, "Christian Denominations." www.religionfacts.com/christianity/branches.

Websites

Religions: Christianity (www.bbc.co.uk/religion/religions/christianity). This British Broadcasting (BBC) site contains links to many topics, including beliefs, history, ethics, rights and rituals, and more. Additional links within each topic area lead to even more detailed information.

Religious Tolerance (www.religioustolerance.org/christ.htm). This site's main page for the topic of Christianity, titled "Christianity: The World's Largest Religion," is the most comprehensive site of its kind on the Internet. The overall site contains thousands of articles that explain the basic facts of all of the world's religions. The writers have backgrounds in several different religions but strive always to be unbiased and accurate.

INDEX

PICTURE CREDITS

ABOUT THE AUTHOR

Historian and award-winning author Don Nardo has written numerous books about the ancient and medieval world, its peoples, and their cultures, including the birth and growth of the major religions in those societies. Nardo, who also composes and arranges orchestral music, lives with his wife, Christine, in Massachusetts.